KINGS & QUEENS

by
John Guy

The Seven Kingdoms

Occupied
□ by Britons

— Boundaries
of Kingdoms

Scotland

Northumbria

North Folk
East Anglia
South Folk
Essex
Kent
Sussex

North Wales
Mercia
Wessex
East Wales

THE KINGDOMS OF ENGLAND

From the departure of the Romans until about 827 England was divided into seven separate kingdoms, known as the Heptarchy. Scotland, Wales and Ireland were also kingdoms in their own right.

📖 ANGLO-SAXON CHRONICLE

In 891 Alfred the Great instigated the compilation of the Anglo-Saxon Chronicle in an attempt to record the history of his newly unified nation. Written in Anglo-Saxon instead of Latin, it gives a brief social and political history of England from before the Roman occupation to the Norman conquest.

EARLY KINGS
SAXON & DANISH KINGS (UP TO 1066)

*U*ntil the 9th century, Britain was a divided land with many separate kingdoms. The area we now know as England was first unified under the rule of Ecgberht (827-39 AD) but peace did not last. Alfred the Great finally united the nation and ruled over all England from AD 886 until his death in AD 899. Succession to the throne in Saxon England did not pass automatically from father to eldest son. The crown was frequently wrested by war or even by murder. In the 11th century, however, things changed. In 1016, the Dane Canute took the throne, ushering in a short period of rule by Danish kings. In 1066 the Normans (or Norse-men) claimed the English crown. They brought stability to the throne and from this point the modern system of numbering the monarchs was introduced.

ECGBERHT (827–39) AND HIS SUCCESSORS

In 802 Ecgberht became King of Wessex, which soon became the most powerful of the Saxon kingdoms. In 827 the other six kings swore allegiance to him and Ecgberht became the first true king of a united England. In 839 he was succeeded by Ethelwulf (839-858), who was later replaced by Ethelbald (858-860), who in turn gave way to Ethelbert (860-866). The last King of Wessex was Aethelred I (866-871).

ALFRED THE GREAT (871–900)

Alfred succeeded to the throne of Wessex in 871 and immediately set about reducing the threat from Viking invaders, who were occupying the north and east of England. Wessex was under constant attack and it was while Alfred was in hiding in Somerset that he was supposed to have famously burned cakes left in his charge. Despite early defeats, Alfred eventually forced the invaders to sign a treaty confining them to an area north of the Wash, known as Danelaw. Then, he set about building fortifications around his kingdom and a naval fleet, earning him the name "Father of the British Navy". Alfred was an exceptional leader and by 886 he was recognised as King of all England. When he died, England remained at war with the Viking invaders for the next 150 years. Alfred was succeeded by Edward the Elder (900-924), Aethelstan (924-940), Edward I (940-946) and Eadred I (946-955).

📖 ARTS & LITERATURE ● BATTLES ⚔ CRIME & PUNISHMENT

EADGAR THE PEACEABLE (959–75)

Eadgar the Peaceable came to the throne at 14 years of age. He was known as the "Peaceable" because his reign was one of prosperity and relative peace with the Vikings. Eadgar's most notable achievement was to restructure the English Church, installing the first Archbishop of Canterbury. He also divided the shires into smaller units of administration known as hundreds, each with its own court. Eadgar was succeeded by Edward the Martyr (975-978).

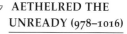

AETHELRED THE UNREADY (978–1016)

Aethelred was a weak monarch who tried to buy off the Vikings by paying them money raised from taxes (known as the Danegeld). However, the Danes eventually forced him to abandon his throne in 1013. Aethelred fled to Normandy for safety, but was later recalled to his old throne at the death of Svein Forkbeard (1013-1014) in 1014. He died in London in 1016.

CANUTE (1016–35)

Peace returned to England under the strong and wise leadership of Canute, a Dane, who was crowned king of England, Denmark and Norway (1016-35). Canute was said to be so powerful that he could command the waves – a claim he dismissed. He took great pains to show his courtiers that the tide could be commanded by no man, as shown in this illustration. Canute was succeeded by the Danes Harold Harefoot (1035-1040) and Harthacanut (1040-1042).

LINE OF SUCCESSION

Saxon & Danish Kings
Ecgberht - 827-839
Ethelwulf - 839-858
Ethelbald - 858-860
Ethelbert - 860-866
Aethelred I - 866-871
Alfred the Great - 871-900
Edward the Elder - 900-924
Aethelstan- 924-940
Edward I - 940-946
Eadred I - 946-955
Eadwy - 955-959
Eadgar the Peaceable - 959-975
Edward the Martyr - 975-978
Aethelred II - 978-1013 & 1014-1016
Sweyn (Dane) - 1013-1014
Edmund Ironside (Dane) - 1016
Canute (Dane) - 1016-1035
Harold Harefoot (Dane) - 1035-1040
Harthacanute (Dane) - 1040-1042
Edward the Confessor - 1042-1066
Harold II - 1066

EDWARD THE CONFESSOR (1042–66)

Edward was known as the Confessor because of his pious nature. He proved to be a strong king, though his preference for Norman advisers incurred the wrath of the Saxon nobility. It led, eventually, to the conquest of England by the Normans.

EXPLORATION   GOVERNMENT   RELIGION

THE NORMANS
1066 ~ 87

dward the Confessor was half-Norman and, until the age of 35, lived with his mother in Normandy. After he became king he often surrounded himself with Norman advisers, and in 1051 he promised the English throne to Duke William of Normandy. On his deathbed, however, Edward stated that his brother-in-law Harold Godwinson, Earl of Wessex, should be king. But in 1064 Harold had sworn allegiance to Duke William, so when he was crowned king, William declared his intention to invade England and take the throne by force.

HAROLD II (1066)

Harold was the son of Godwin, Earl of Wessex, whose sister Edith had married Edward the Confessor. An ongoing dispute had led, in 1051, to the Godwin family being banished from England. They were restored to their estates the following year and in 1053 Harold became the king's chief adviser. He persuaded Edward to renege on his promise to pass the crown to Duke William and had himself proclaimed king on Edward's death on 5th January 1066. It was to be a short-lived reign.

THE CLAIMANT TO THE THRONE

The Normans, or "Norse-men", were originally Vikings who settled in an area of northern France in the early 10th century. They built up a domain that rivalled the power of the king of France. William was the illegitimate son of Robert, Duke of Normandy, and he succeeded to the dukedom in 1035 when only eight years old. He extended his empire until it covered much of western Europe and is said never to have engaged in a fight he did not win.

THE BATTLE OF HASTINGS

The battle took place on 14th October 1066 about six miles north of Hastings on an escarpment known as Senlac Hill. The armies of both Harold and William were evenly matched, though the Saxons were tired from their long march south following a previous battle, the Battle of Stamford Bridge. The Saxons occupied the top of the ridge and successfully held off the Norman advances. Late in the day, William ordered his men to feign a retreat. The Saxons gave chase and lost the advantage of the high ground, leaving them at the mercy of the Norman archers and cavalry. The Normans were victorious but though Harold sustained a fatal injury, it is not certain that he actually died on the battlefield.

📖 ARTS & LITERATURE   🔴 BATTLES   ⚖ CRIME & PUNISHMENT

BAYEUX TAPESTRY

Odo, Bishop of Bayeux and half brother of Duke William, is believed to have commissioned the Bayeux Tapestry. It is a huge needlework tableau depicting the events leading up to, and following, the Battle of Hastings.

WILLIAM I (1066–87) - THE CONQUEROR

Following his victory at Hastings, on 14th October 1066, William then marched on London, putting down local opposition as he went. He was crowned on Christmas Day the same year in Westminster Abbey. William subdued the Saxons by systematically confiscating their lands and giving them to his Norman supporters, almost destroying the Saxon nobility in the process. He was a fair but uncompromising ruler, who could be ruthless and brutal. He died after falling from his horse during a military campaign in France. William's lasting legacy is the Domesday book, an astonishing achievement and a lasting record of medieval England.

THE FEUDAL SYSTEM

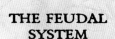

THE KING

owned all the land which he granted to:

DUKES & EARLS

in exchange for military service and advice. They then let the land to:

LESSER BARONS

in exchange for military service and advice. They then tenanted the land, known as "a knights fee" to:

KNIGHTS

in exchange for military service and supply of foot soldiers. The knights sub-let the land to Norman and Saxon:

FARMERS

who worked the land in exchange for military service from foot soldiers.

All owed first allegiance to the King and then to their respective overlords, to whom they also paid rents.

THE FEUDAL SYSTEM

One of the first things William did on becoming king was to reorganise the governmental structure of England with the introduction of the feudal system. Under these new rules, all land was held by the king and sub-tenanted to his most loyal lords. They in turn sub-let their holdings and so on, down to tenant farmers. All owed allegiance to their immediate overlord, and ultimately the king, who could call upon them at any time to do military service.

THE DOMESDAY BOOK

In 1085 William ordered the compilation of a great survey of his newly conquered land. Completed in just one year and covering most of the country, it records in minute detail the land ownership and uses of almost every village and estate. The population of England at that time was recorded as two million. Compiled in two huge volumes, the Domesday Book still exists today.

THE NORMANS
1087 ~1154

hen William I died his lands were divided between his two eldest sons. Robert inherited Normandy, while William became king of England. Although, as invaders, none of the Norman kings were popular with the Saxon population, William I had at least been a strong and just ruler. His son William was more ruthless and less judicial than his father, however. He never married and on his death the throne passed to his younger brother, Henry.

WILLIAM II (1087–1100)

William (left) was known as "Rufus" because of the reddish colour of his hair and complexion. He was extravagent and openly took money from the church, but it was the actions of his mercenary soldiers that attracted most criticism. Villagers were said to desert their homes when the king's entourage approached, rather than submit to their brutality. William was killed by a stray arrow while hunting in the New Forest in August 1100. The circumstances of his death were suspicious, but because he was so disliked, little attempt was made to solve the mystery. Chief among the suspects was Henry, William I's youngest son. He was in the vicinity at the time and on hearing news rode straight to London to declare himself king.

CLAIM TO THE THRONE

The rightful heir to the English throne on William II's death was his brother Robert, Duke of Normandy. When Henry proclaimed himself king three days later, Robert invaded England to claim the throne. He failed, however and was imprisoned by Henry, who then seized Robert's lands in Normandy.

HENRY I (1100–35)

Henry was a calculating and shrewd man who knew he had to placate the Saxon population to strengthen his position. On succeeding to the throne he married Edith, the daughter of Malcolm III of Scotland, uniting the two countries. He also introduced several legal reforms, including an improved judiciary, and issued a Charter of Liberties promising to govern well and fairly, treating Saxon and Norman equally. In the main, Henry's reign was peaceful, but he was in constant fear of assassination and slept with his sword by his side. When he eventually died in 1135, it is believed to have been from seafood poisoning.

 ARTS & LITERATURE　　 BATTLES　　 CRIME & PUNISHMENT

TRAGEDY STRIKES

The "White Ship", reputedly the finest vessel of its day, ran aground and sank in the Channel in November 1120, while returning from Normandy. Henry's only legitimate son and heir, William, drowned in the accident caused, it is believed, by a drunken crew. His death left the crown without a male heir. Henry spent the last years of his reign persuading the barons to swear allegiance to his daughter, Matilda. However, Henry's nephew Stephen also claimed the throne on the grounds that as William I's eldest surviving grandson, he was the rightful heir.

STEPHEN (1135–54)

Stephen had sworn his allegiance to Matilda as heir to the throne, along with most other barons. When Henry I died, however, Aethelred usurped the throne and had himself crowned king. Almost the entire duration of his reign was spent in civil war as the barons divided their allegiance between him and Matilda. Although a good-natured and courteous man, Stephen was also weak. A state of anarchy developed during his reign during which the barons plundered the country at will while, it was said, "Christ and His saints slept".

MATILDA

Matilda was born in 1102 to Henry I and Edith of Scotland. She was arrogant, had a fiery temper and a quite objectionable nature that caused many of her allies to desert her. In 1129 she married Geoffrey Plantagenet, Count of Anjou. Their son ruled England as Henry II, so beginning a new royal dynasty – the Plantagenets.

TIMELINE OF THE CIVIL WAR

1135
Stephen usurps the throne from Matilda.

1136
Civil war breaks out between barons who support either Stephen or Matilda.

1138
David I of Scotland invades England in support of his niece, Matilda, but is defeated at the Battle of Standard.

1139
Matilda returns to England from France to claim the throne.

1141
Stephen captured at the Battle of Lincoln, and is imprisoned at Bristol Castle. Matilda rules for 6 months, but is not crowned.

1142
Siege of Oxford Castle, where Matilda is besieged for 3 months. She escapes but her garrison is starved into submission.

1145
Stephen defeats Matilda at the Battle of Farringdon.

1148
Matilda concedes defeat and flees to Anjou, France.

1151
Matilda's son Henry succeeds his father as Count of Anjou.

1153
Henry re-opens civil war with Stephen.

1153
Stephen agrees to pass throne to Henry on his death at the Treaty of Westminster.

TREATY OF WESTMINSTER

In 1153 Henry of Anjou, Matilda's son, took up the claim for the English throne where his mother had left off. Henry quickly gathered support and at the Treaty of Westminster it was agreed that Stephen should remain king until his death, but then the throne should pass to Henry, and not to Stephen's heirs. This brought 19 years of civil war to an end.

 EXPLORATION GOVERNMENT ✝ RELIGION

THE PLANTAGENETS
1154 ~1399

*f*ollowing the turmoil of Stephen's reign, England needed a strong king to re-unite a divided nation. It found him in Henry II, the son of Matilda and Geoffrey Plantagenet. So began a dynasty that was to last for over 300 years. The Plantagenets were a hugely powerful family not just in England but throughout Europe.

HENRY II (1154–89)

Henry came to the throne at just 21, a strong and well-educated man. Despite a fiery temper, he was a just king who ruled well and introduced many legal reforms, including trial by jury. In 1164 he attempted to curb the power of the church in England, a move opposed by the Archbishop, Thomas Becket. This opposition led to Becket's murder in Canterbury Cathedral. In 1166, Henry sent an army to Ireland following an appeal by one of the Irish kings to help him crush opposition by the other Irish chieftains. Five years later Henry invaded Ireland himself, proclaiming himself Lord of Ireland. Now his empire was larger than any other king before him. It included England, Wales, Ireland, Normandy, Anjou, Brittany and Aquitaine.

 UNHAPPY FAMILIES

In 1152 Henry married Eleanor of Aquitaine, but his family life was far from happy. Between 1173-4 his sons Henry, Geoffrey, Richard and John rebelled against him, encouraged by Eleanor. The king put down the rebellion and kept Eleanor a virtual prisoner for the last 15 years of his reign.

RICHARD I (1189–99)

Richard I was the third and eldest surviving son of Henry II. He is usually depicted as a brave, warrior king, and was given the nickname "Lionheart". Richard spent barely seven months of his 10 year reign in England and spoke little English. England was merely a source of revenue to finance his Crusades abroad.

His queen, Berengaria of Navarre, never set foot in England. On his return from the Holy Lands, Richard was imprisoned by Henry VI, Emperor of Germany, who demanded a huge ransom for his safe return. The ransom was raised, mostly through taxation in England, leaving the country almost bankrupt. Richard returned to England briefly, before departing for France, where he died leaving no heir.

 SCOTTISH INDEPENDENCE
In 1173–4, William the Lion, King of Scotland, unsuccessfully invaded England. He was captured by Henry II and surrendered Scottish sovereignty to the English monarch. However, he purchased Scotland's independence back again in 1189 for a cash payment to Richard I, who needed fund the Crusades. A peace treaty acknowledging Scotland's independence was signed in 1217.

✞ THE CRUSADES

The Crusades were a series of nine religious wars waged from 1095 to liberate the Holy Land from Islamic rule. They proved Richard to be a competent soldier and also a very cruel man. During the Third Crusade, he ordered 2,700 captured Muslims to be executed.

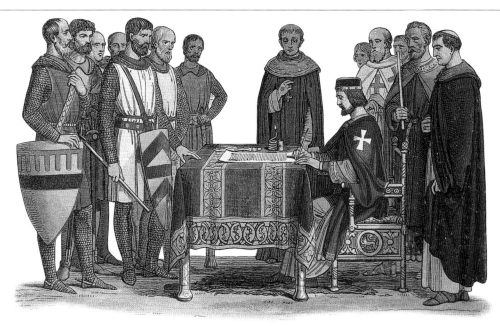

JOHN (1199–1216)

John was, in truth, a much better king than history has portrayed him. Although he was implicated in a plot to usurp the crown from his brother, many of the problems John faced were caused by Richard I's neglect of England. The cost of the Crusades and Richard's ransom had meant that he inherited a near bankrupt country with a dissatisfied nobility. England accepted John as king, but the barons in France regarded Arthur, John's nephew, to be the rightful heir. War broke out between the two countries, and by 1204 John had lost virtually all his French lands. The conflict between John and his English barons had been building up over many years. High taxation, disputes with the church, tampering with the legal system, and the loss of the French domains all culminated in civil war. Violence only ended with John's death from a fever in 1216.

MAGNA CARTA

The barons forced John to sign the Great Charter at Runneymede on 15th June 1215. It outlined the rights and responsibilities of the crown and the nobles, with the king only allowed to govern within the confines of the charter. Mostly the charter was specific to the barons and the rights of the church – it had little effect on the lives of ordinary people – but it is now regarded as a milestone in our constitutional history.

HENRY III (1216–72)

Henry was only nine years old when his father, John, died. Perhaps anticipating his demise, John had already made provision for two people called regents to rule until Henry became old enough to take control in 1227. But years of misrule eventually led to civil war again – largely because of the embittered relationship with the barons, inherited from his father. Leading the civil war was Simon de Montfort, who became known as "father of English Parliament". He was determined to make government accountable and open to all classes. He defeated Henry in 1264 and called the first open English Parliament. Despite these problems, Henry's continued to reign as king, his rule marked by many advancements in architecture and the arts.

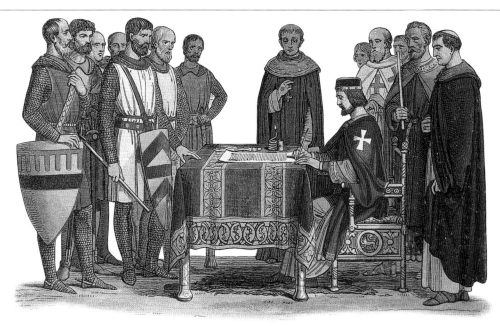

EXPLORATION   GOVERNMENT   RELIGION

EDWARD I (1272–1307)

Edward "Longshanks" (so-called because he was over 6 ft tall) was an athletic, handsome man with a slight speech impediment. He was away on the Eighth Crusade to the Holy Land with his uncle, Louis IX of France, when he heard of his father's death. The crusade failed and Edward returned home to be crowned king, in August 1274. He was a formidable soldier who spent much of his reign trying to unite England, Scotland and Wales into one kingdom. In 1277 he launched an invasion of the latter, but the people of north Wales managed to hold out against him until 1284. Edward was a very able and just ruler, responsible for many political and social reforms, including the creation of the first democratically elected parliament. It was called the "Model Parliament" and it made up of lords, knights, clergy and representatives from the shires and towns.

WILLIAM WALLACE

In 1290 the Scottish throne fell vacant. A successor could not be agreed so Edward I chose John Balliol, a man whom Edward thought could be manipulated. But in 1295, Balliol formed an alliance with France against England. The following year Edward I invaded Scotland, deposed Balliol and proclaimed himself King of Scotland. Led by William Wallace (above), the Scots rebelled and defeated Edward at the Battle of Stirling Bridge. Edward re-invaded Scotland but Wallace continued to lead the revolt until 1305, when he was betrayed and captured. He was hung, drawn and quartered, and parts of his body were sent to all four corners of the kingdom

ROBERT BRUCE (1306-29)

Following Wallace's execution, Robert Bruce declared himself leader of the rebels against English rule, even though he had originally offered his support to Edward. He was crowned Robert I, King of Scotland, in 1306. The following year, Edward re-invaded but Bruce hit back and attacked Stirling Castle in 1314, defeating the English. Despite his victory, Scotland did not gain full independence until 1327.

EDWARD II (1307–27)

Edward II (below) was the fourth, but eldest surviving son of Edward I. Although often dismissed as an inept administrator, England actually prospered during his rule. While his father had raised taxes considerably to pay for his wars in Wales and Scotland, Edward looked to reduce them. He married Isabella of France in 1308 and she bore him four children, but it was a loveless marriage. In 1326, Isabella and her lover, Roger Mortimer, led a rebellion, forcing Edward's deposition in favour of his son. Whilst held prisoner, Edward formally abdicated. He was later murdered on the instructions of Isabella.

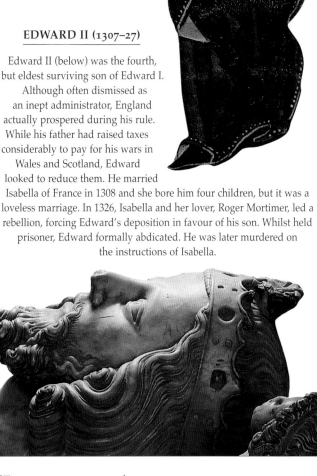

EDWARD III (1327–77)

Edward came to the throne at the age of 14. For the first three years, the country was governed by his mother, Isabella, and her lover, Roger Mortimer. In 1330 Edward seized power for himself and set about righting some of the wrongs that had been directed towards his father. He removed Isabella from office and Mortimer was executed for his crimes. Edward was an heroic figure like his grandfather, popular with the people because of his just government and dashing victories on the battlefield. He was the epitome of the chivalrous medieval king. In 1348 he founded the Order of the Garter, an band of knights who took their inspiration directly from the epic tales of King Arthur and the knights of the Round Table. Edward was devoted to his wife, Philippa of Hainault, until her death in 1369. Edward died eight years after Philippa, probably from senile dementia.

🔥 100 YEARS' WAR

Edward claimed the throne of France through his French mother, Isabella, marking the beginning of the 100 Years' War with France. The wars consisted of a series of battles during the period 1337–1453. The English had several early successes, but gradually the tide of the wars changed, with the French finally evicting the English in 1453 at the Battle of Châtillon.

THE BLACK PRINCE

Edward III's eldest son was also called Edward. He was known as the Black Prince because of the colour of his armour. Edward won his spurs at the Battle of Crecy in 1346 when just 16 years old, and soon became the most feared warrior in Europe. He died the year before his father in 1376 at the age of 46.

RICHARD II (1377–1399)

Richard II was the son of Edward the Black Prince. His father had been a popular hero and so Richard was destined, perhaps, to be forever in his shadow. There were also those who thought the throne should have passed to one of Edward III's other sons – John of Gaunt, or his son Henry Bolingbroke. Until 1389 the country was ruled by advisers, during which time there were several periods of social unrest. Although Richard ruled well for a while, he was a sickly man, more interested in art and music than government. When Henry Bolingbroke returned from exile in in 1399 to reclaim his inheritance, Richard was behaving irrationally and had incurred the wrath of his barons. Bolingbroke forced him to abdicate on the grounds of his misrule and imprisoned the king in Pontefract Castle, where he died in suspicious circumstances.

⚑ EXPLORATION   📜 GOVERNMENT   ✝ RELIGION

HENRY IV (1399–1413)

As a young man, Henry travelled throughout Europe and the Middle East, fighting alongside the Teutonic Knights, an order of religious knights. He was valiant and a good leader, but his reign was unremarkable. Henry was plagued with illness and faced many rebellions. Most notable of these were the Welsh uprisings led by Owain Glyndwr, which continued throughout Henry's reign. The king also faced a revolt from the Percys, who had previously been among his most loyal supporters. This dispute ended in the defeat of Henry Percy (Harry Hotspur) at the Battle of Shrewsbury. Henry is believed to have contracted leprosy, or a similar debilitating disease, in 1406. He died of a seizure in 1413 aged just 46.

THE PLANTAGENETS
THE HOUSE OF LANCASTER
(1399~1471)

Henry Bolingbroke came to the English throne by force. He made his cousin, Richard II, abdicate, and then seized the crown himself. But Henry's debatable claim to the throne was to start a dispute between the House of Lancaster (the descendants of John of Gaunt) and the House of York (the descendants of John's brother Edmund, Duke of York). Both were separate branches of the Plantagenet dynasty but their dispute caused its demise. It eventually led to the Wars of the Roses, which ended in 1485 when Henry Tudor claimed the throne.

HENRY V (1413–22)

Henry V became king in 1413, at the age of 25. One of his first acts was to pursue a claim to the French throne. The continuation of the 100 Years' War with France served the dual purpose of extending his military prowess and unifying a divided nobility against a common enemy. At the "Treaty of Troyes" in 1420, Henry forced the French king, Charles VI (considered by many to be mad), to make him his heir and regent of France. Henry also requested the hand of Charles's daughter, Katherine, in marriage. They were married later the same year, thus briefly uniting the crowns of England and France. Henry might have gone down in history as one of our greatest monarchs but for his untimely and premature death at the age of 35. Had he lived a few weeks longer, he would have inherited the French throne.

📖 **SHAKESPEARE'S HERO**
William Shakespeare's fictional Histories are plays chronicling the lives of the Plantagenet kings. Shakespeare is responsible for the image of Henry V as a heroic and saintly king (left).

📖 ARTS & LITERATURE　　🌢 BATTLES　　⚖ CRIME & PUNISHMENT

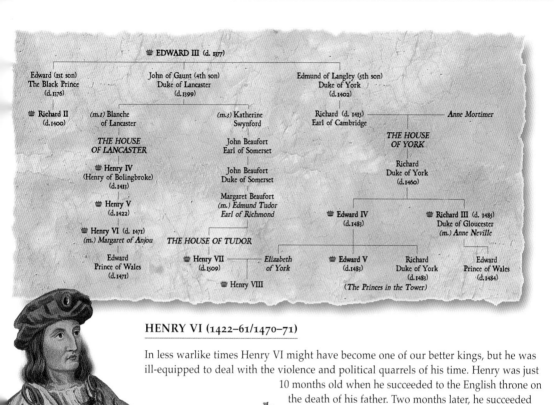

♛ EDWARD III (d. 1377)

Edward (1st son)
The Black Prince
(d. 1376)

John of Gaunt (4th son)
Duke of Lancaster
(d. 1399)

Edmund of Langley (5th son)
Duke of York
(d. 1402)

♛ Richard II
(d. 1400)

(m.1) Blanche
of Lancaster

(m.3) Katherine
Swynford

Richard (d. 1415)
Earl of Cambridge — Anne Mortimer

THE HOUSE
OF LANCASTER

John Beaufort
Earl of Somerset

THE HOUSE
OF YORK

♛ Henry IV
(Henry of Bolingbroke)
(d. 1413)

John Beaufort
Duke of Somerset

Richard
Duke of York
(d. 1460)

♛ Henry V
(d. 1422)

Margaret Beaufort
(m.) Edmund Tudor
Earl of Richmond

♛ Edward IV
(d. 1483)

♛ Richard III (d. 1485)
Duke of Gloucester
(m.) Anne Neville

♛ Henry VI (d. 1471)
(m.) Margaret of Anjou

THE HOUSE OF TUDOR

Edward
Prince of Wales
(d. 1471)

♛ Henry VII — Elizabeth
(d. 1509)   of York

♛ Edward V
(d. 1483)

Richard
Duke of York
(d. 1483)

Edward
Prince of Wales
(d. 1484)

♛ Henry VIII

(The Princes in the Tower)

HENRY VI (1422–61/1470–71)

In less warlike times Henry VI might have become one of our better kings, but he was ill-equipped to deal with the violence and political quarrels of his time. Henry was just 10 months old when he succeeded to the English throne on the death of his father. Two months later, he succeeded to the French throne on the death of his grandfather, Charles VI. Henry took over governance of both kingdoms at the age of just 15. A gentle, well-educated and devoutly religious man, he had a naive, almost unworldly nature that was seen as a weakness by his enemies and his dominating wife. Henry suffered from bouts of mental illness – the first in 1454, when his cousin Richard, Duke of York, was made Protector of England. Richard rebelled when Henry tried to dismiss him, marking the beginning of the War of the Roses. Henry was deposed in 1461 and replaced on the throne by Richard's son, who ruled as Edward IV until 1470. Henry was briefly reinstated but was overthrown again in 1471 and sent to the Tower of London, where he was murdered while at prayer.

🕊 WARS OF THE ROSES
Although usually described as a civil war, the Wars of the Roses were, more correctly, a dynastic struggle between two families with rival claims to the throne. They were really a series of intermittent battles that took place over a period of 30 years between the private armies of the claimants, and did not affect the everyday lives of the majority of the population.

 EXPLORATION   GOVERNMENT   ✝ RELIGION

THE PLANTAGENETS
THE HOUSE OF YORK
1471~85

Edward IV came to the throne in 1461 after defeating Henry VI at the Battle of Towton, in Yorkshire. He was just 19 years old. He is generally considered to have had a stronger claim to the throne than Henry VI, but battles continued to rage between the two families.

EDWARD IV (1461–1470/1471–1483)

Edward was said to be about 6 ft 3 inches tall, a giant for the time. He began his reign as a genial, well-mannered diplomat, but when he died suddenly at the age of 40 he was accused of living a life of debauchery and excess. Edward was helped to the throne by Richard, Earl of Warwick, known as "the Kingmaker", but in 1470 Warwick switched his allegiance to Henry VI. Edward was forced to flee into exile in Flanders, and Warwick helped Henry VI return to the throne briefly. Eventually Edward returned from exile to reassert his claim. A bloody battle was fought at Barnet in Hertfordshire on Easter Day, 1471, and Edward was restored to the throne.

ENGLAND PROSPERS
Edward IV was determined to restore peace and economic stability. He did a great deal to aid English merchants and helped England enjoy the greatest period of prosperity the country had ever witnessed.

THE TWO PRINCES
The last recorded sighting of the two princes (right) was in the gardens of the Tower of London – then the principal royal palace. They are believed to have been suffocated by unknown assailants in the Bloody Tower, so named after the deed. Two children's bodies were found in the Tower in 1674, but their identities have never been confirmed.

DUKE OF CLARENCE

Edward's brother George, Duke of Clarence, had several times switched his allegiance, but Edward had always forgiven him. However, after a furious argument in 1478, George was imprisoned in the Tower for treason.

EDWARD V (1483)

When Edward IV died, the throne passed to his eldest son Prince Edward. He became Edward V at the age of just 13. Edward's uncle Richard, Duke of Gloucester, was appointed Protector during the king's minority. Because Edward's father had already been bethrothed to another at the time of his marriage to Elizabeth Woodville, however, the marriage was declared invalid. In June 1483 Parliament declared Edward V (and his brother) illegitimate and deposed the king in favour of his uncle, who became Richard III. It was deemed that Edward IV's brother, Richard was therefore the rightful heir. After Richard was proclaimed king, Edward and his brother disappeared without trace, one of history's great mysteries.

ARTS & LITERATURE · BATTLES · CRIME & PUNISHMENT

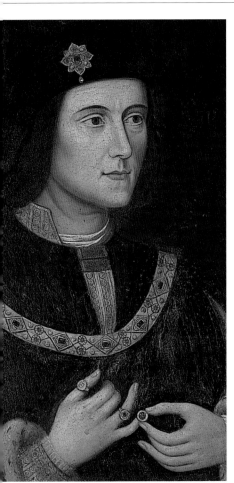

RICHARD III (1483–85)

Richard III has always been the prime suspect in the suspected murder of the two princes, but was never accused in his lifetime. He is perhaps the most maligned king in British history, largely as a result of the political propaganda put about by the Tudors. Richard was tall, quite handsome and popular with the people. However, his reign was soon over. He was killed during the Battle of Bosworth Field, a battle between Richard's and Henry Tudor's armies, bringing an end to the Wars of the Roses and the House of York.

📖 SHAKESPEARE'S IMAGE

Shakespeare portrayed Richard III as a hideous hunchback, a monstrous tyrant and murderer of his nephews. Shakespeare based his play on books written by Henry VII's supporters who aimed to justify their seizure of the crown.

ANNE NEVILLE

Richard married Anne Neville in 1472. She was the daughter of Richard Neville, Earl of Warwick. Before Warwick's change of allegiance, their two families had been very close and they were allegedly childhood sweethearts. She died in 1485 shortly before Richard's death in battle at Bosworth.

⚔ BATTLE OF BOSWORTH FIELD

The Battle of Bosworth took place in a field outside the Leicestershire town of Market Bosworth on 22nd August 1485. Henry Tudor's army of between 7-8,000 faced a superior force of about 11-12,000. The battle could have gone either way, but when Richard III himself was killed, his supporters drifted away, leaving the Lancastrian Henry Tudor the victor. The battle brought to a bloody end the "Wars of the Roses" and the Plantagent dynasty itself.

THE EARLY STUARTS (1406-1513)

The Stuart dynasty asserted their claim to the Scottish throne in 1371, on the death of David II. David's nephew, Robert Stewart, who was the High Steward of Scotland and grandson of Robert Bruce, became the first Stuart monarch (the family later adopted the French spelling of Stuart). The Stuarts were a powerful, ambitious family who were great patrons of the arts and brought Scotland to the forefront of cultural developments in Europe.

JAMES I (1406–37)
Held prisoner for 18 years by Henry IV, James returned to Scotland as king in 1424. Popular with the people, but unpopular with the barons, he was assasinated in 1437.

JAMES II (1437–60)
Continuing his father's work to quell the powers of the barons, he also fought valiantly to control the clans. James II was a great patron of learning and the arts, establishing Glasgow university.

JAMES III (1460–88)
When James II died suddenly, the throne passed to his nine-year-old son, James III. He assumed personal control in 1470, and was pious and well-educated, but not a military man.

JAMES IV (1488–1513)
An able administrator, James IV established Scotland as a truly united and independent nation. In 1503, he married Margaret Tudor, Henry VII's daughter, thus briefly uniting the two countries.

 EXPLORATION 📜 GOVERNMENT ✝ RELIGION

THE TUDORS
1485~1603

*T*he Tudor period was more than just the start of a new dynasty. It marked the end of the Middle Ages. Under Henry VII's rule society changed quite radically, casting off many of the feudal ideals in favour of commercial ones. The "Wars of the Roses" had severely weakened the grip of the nobility and Henry took advantage of the situation by promoting business enterprise and encouraging merchants to expand their interests. His policies certainly worked and England prospered under Henry's leadership.

⌖ CHRISTOPHER COLUMBUS

Christopher Columbus approached Henry for patronage when he embarked upon his voyages of discovery in the "New World". Henry was keen to develop business interests outside of war-torn Europe and considered sponsoring Columbus who, in 1492, re-discovered America.

⌖ THE NEW WORLD

Unshackled by the old ideals, the Tudor age really was an age of adventure. Henry was keen to patronise anyone who might further England's prosperity by opening up new trade routes. From 1496 on, Henry sponsored John Cabot (a Venetian who had settled in England) and his three sons to seek out new lands, in return for which he demanded one-fifth of any profits.

HENRY VII (1485–1509)

Henry was the grandson of Owen Tudor, who claimed to be descended from the independent Princes of Wales. His mother was great-granddaughter of John of Gaunt, through whom Henry claimed the English throne. It was a weak claim and so Henry set about to establish his credibility. He conducted a successful smear campaign to blacken the name of Richard III, and may himself have been responsible for the murders of Edward V and his brother. Within six months of acceding to the throne, Henry (a Lancastrian) married Elizabeth of York, uniting the two warring families and so bringing to an end 30 years of civil war. Henry was a great patron of the arts and encouraged the English Renaissance among artists and scholars in the relative peace of his reign.

ARTHUR, PRINCE OF WALES

Prince Arthur was the eldest son of Henry VII and had been groomed for kingship. He married Catherine of Aragon, the Spanish king's daughter, to unite the two countries. Arthur died, prematurely, in 1502. When Henry died, the crown passed to his second son, Henry, who also married Catherine to maintain the alliance.

HENRY VIII (1509–47)

Henry VIII came to the throne at the age of 17. He was a flamboyant character, well liked at first, but he became something of a tyrant in later years, particularly if he did not get his own way. Despite being one of our more well-known monarchs, he was not a great king and is best remembered for breaking with the Church of Rome and for marrying six times. Henry was plagued by ill-health in later years. He suffered from severe headaches, smallpox, syphilis, thrombosis and ulcerated legs. He was also grossly overweight, and had to be carried up and down stairs using a hoist.

📖 ARTS & LITERATURE   ✦ BATTLES   ⚖ CRIME & PUNISHMENT

THE SIX WIVES OF HENRY VIII

Henry VIII married six times, the first three of which were said to be genuine love matches. The last three were purely political or for reasons of expediency. He had been happily married to Catherine of Aragon for the first 20 years of his reign, and married all of the other five within the last 11 years.

1. CATHERINE OF ARAGON

Born 1485 • Married 1509 • Divorced 1533 • Died 1536

Catherine of Aragon was beautiful, intelligent and fun-loving. She married Henry VIII's brother, Arthur, but was widowed within six months. In 1509 she married Henry and they remained happily married for 20 years. They had several children but only one, Princess Mary, survived. It was only after Catherine's inability to conceive a son and heir for Henry that he tried to have the marriage annulled. The pope denied Henry so he broke with the Church of Rome and divorced her in 1533.

2. ANNE BOLEYN

Born 1502 • Married 1533 • Divorced 1536 • Executed 1536

When it became clear that Catherine could not give him a son, Henry began to take mistresses, including the queen's lady-in-waiting, Anne Boleyn. They married in secret, four months before his divorce from Catherine. Anne gave birth to Princess Elizabeth the same year. When Anne too failed to give him a son, Henry started divorce proceedings. She was accused of adultery and the marriage was annulled. Two days later Anne was executed in the Tower of London.

3. JANE SEYMOUR

Born 1509 • Married 1536 • Died 1537

Henry began to cast his eye towards Anne's lady-in-waiting, Jane Seymour. At first Jane declined his advances but they were married two weeks after Anne's execution. The following year, Jane gave birth to a son, Edward, but she died of blood poisoning two weeks later. Henry was heartbroken.

4. ANNE OF CLEVES

Born 1515 • Married 1540 • Divorced 1540 • Died 1557

Following Jane's death Henry might not have married again, but he faced mounting political pressure to find a new partner. Reluctantly he agreed to a marriage of convenience to the German princess, Anne of Cleves. Henry disliked her intensely, calling her the "Flanders Mare", and refused to consummate the marriage. They were divorced just six months later.

5. CATHERINE HOWARD

Born 1521 • Married 1540 • Executed 1542

Henry took an instant liking to Anne of Cleves' lady servant, Catherine Howard. She was high-spirited and flirtatious, which at first aroused Henry's interest, but later was the cause of his jealousy. Less than two years after their marriage, she was executed at just 21, accused of adultery, unseemly behaviour and treason.

6. CATHERINE PARR

Born 1512 • Married 1543 • Died 1548

Catherine Parr was a quiet, well-educated lady of comparatively mature years, in stark contrast to her predecessors. Henry was by that time suffering from several serious ailments and Catherine acted more as a nurse towards him than a wife. She survived Henry to marry again, but died in childbirth.

PERSECUTIONS

As Henry's reign wore on he became ever more obsessive and tyrannical. He removed from office anyone who stood in his way and ordered the executions of several thousand people - one estimate puts the figure as high as 50,000!

BREAK WITH THE CHURCH OF ROME

There was a growing band of people, called Protestants, who disagreed with many of the Catholic doctrines and who sought church reforms. When the pope refused to annul Henry's marriage to Catherine of Aragon, the Protestants seized upon the opportunity to establish a new church and lent their support to the king. Although England eventually broke away from the Church of Rome, Henry himself remained a Catholic.

EXPLORATION   GOVERNMENT   RELIGION

EDWARD VI (1547–1553)

Edward succeeded to the throne at the age of nine as the only surviving legitimate son of Henry VIII. Until about the age of five or six he was brought up in the royal nursery, with his half-sister, Elizabeth, but from then on he was groomed for his future role as king. Before he was old enough to be crowned king the country was governed on his behalf by an older person called a protector, but on his coronation Edward became the first Protestant monarch of England. Under his rule the Reformation of the English Church was consolidated. Edward was a sickly child with many of his father's arrogant mannerisms. In January 1553 he contracted tuberculosis and died six months later, aged just 15.

LADY JANE GREY

Lady Jane Grey is one of the tragic figures of English history. She was the Protestant daughter of Frances, Duchess of Suffolk, and Henry VIII's great-niece. An intelligent, quiet and beautiful girl, she became a good friend to Edward, her cousin. When Edward lay on his deathbed he was persuaded to name Jane as his successor to ensure that the throne remained in Protestant hands. Jane reluctantly agreed, but ruled for just nine days before being taken prisoner by Mary, Edward's half-sister and rightful heir. Lady Jane Grey was executed the following year when just 17 years old.

MARY I (1553–1558)

Mary I was probably one of England's most unpopular monarchs. She was the daughter of Henry VIII by his first wife, the Spaniard Catherine of Aragon, and was brought up a devout Catholic. Mary became embittered when her parents divorced and her accession to the throne was denied. She also refused to acknowledge her half-sister, Princess Elizabeth. When Edward VI died in 1553, Mary was again passed over in favour of Lady Jane Grey. Not to be denied this time, however, she marched on London and deposed Jane. Under her rule Protestants were cruelly persecuted and many were burned at the stake for heresy, earning the queen the title, "Bloody Mary".

KING PHILIP OF SPAIN

Mary married Philip of Spain in July 1554, partly to form an alliance with Spain and partly to strengthen the return to Catholicism. It was an unhappy marriage and produced no children. Philip spent little time with Mary in England, and when he succeeded to the Spanish throne in 1556, he left England and never returned.

📖 ARTS & LITERATURE   💣 BATTLES   ⚖ CRIME & PUNISHMENT

ELIZABETH 1 (1558–1603)

The daughter of Henry VIII and Anne Boleyn, Elizabeth was third in line to the throne and could never have expected to become queen. Her reign began when she was 25 and was marked by its stability, successfully uniting a bitterly divided country. It was an age of adventure and discovery and England prospered as never before, laying the foundations of the British Empire. England's naval commanders were becoming daring and proficient, posing a very real threat to the might of Spain, then the most powerful country in Europe. Elizabeth further inflamed relations between the two countries by turning down a marriage proposal from her brother-in-law, Philip II of Spain. This rebuff gave Philip the perfect excuse to lead an invasion to try to re-establish papal authority in England. The unsuccessful Armada was a humiliating defeat for Spain, but England's victory established a sense of national pride. As Elizabeth's status grew throughout Europe, England came to be recognised as a growing world power.

DRAKE's CIRCUMNAVIGATION

Francis Drake circumnavigated the world between 1577-80, the first Englishman to do so. On his return he was greeted with a hero's welcome and was knighted by Elizabeth aboard his ship, the "Golden Hind" (shown above).

ACT OF SUPREMACY

An Act of Supremacy, passed in 1559, re-established the monarchy as Supreme Head of the Church in England, following Mary's attempts to re-establish papal authority in England.

THE SPANISH ARMADA

Spain sent a massive armada in 1588 as the first stage in a proposed invasion of England. However, the daring seamanship of Drake, Frobisher, Hawkins and others outmanoeuvred the Spanish fleet, which was routed in a week-long running battle in the Channel. Of 138 ships that set out from Spain, only 67 returned, escaping only by sailing north around the coasts of Scotland and Ireland.

THE VIRGIN QUEEN

Elizabeth never married. She chose instead to remain a virgin and devote her life to governing the country. She once said that she was married to the "Kingdom of England". When her glorious reign came to an end in 1603, Elizabeth died childless and so the Tudor dynasty came to an end.

MARY QUEEN OF SCOTS

The Tudors were related to the Stuarts, royal family of Scotland. Elizabeth's cousin Mary, a Catholic and queen of Scotland, was involved in a plot to place her on the English throne. Aware that Mary had been implicated against her will, Elizabeth was reluctant to sign her death warrant, but after 19 years of imprisonment, she grudgingly authorized her death warrent in 1587. Elizabeth never married and so when she died, the throne passed to the Scottish Stuart family, and to Mary's son, James VI of Scotland (James I of England), Elizabeth's closest relative.

THE POOR LAW

In 1601 a Poor Law was passed in Parliament which imposed a poor relief rate on the wealthy to help keep those who could not work because they were blind, sick or crippled. Those who were capable of work, but chose to live as vagabonds, were punished. Poor people receiving relief had to stay within their own parish.

 EXPLORATION   GOVERNMENT   RELIGION

19

THE STUARTS

1603 ~1714

The Stuarts were a great and powerful Scottish dynasty who ruled an independent Scotland. When Elizabeth I of England died, James VI of Scotland was crowned King James I of England. He united both countries and the Stuart dynasty continued, stronger and even more powerful than before.

JAMES I (1603–25)

James succeeded to the Scottish throne when just a few months old. When he was crowned King James I of England, he had ruled Scotland for 36 years, under the doctrine of the "Divine Right of Kings". This maintained that kings were appointed by God and were beyond judgement. For the English this was unacceptable – Parliament had long campaigned to reduce the power of the monarchy and when James ruled for long periods without Parliament he became increasingly unpopular. He was, by all accounts, a small and ungainly man with a speech impediment caused by having a tongue too large for his mouth. His manners and personal hygiene were atrocious, and although well-educated, he seemed unable to focus either his wit or his intelligence. James earned the nickname "the wisest fool in Christendom" because of his heavy reliance on his advisers. They included George Villiers, the Duke of Buckingham, who became so powerful that, as the king sank into senility in later life, he virtually ruled the country unaided.

THE PILGRIM FATHERS

James told the Puritans (an extra zealous group of Protestants) that if they did not conform to the Church of England they would be "harried from the land". A small group of them, unwilling to conform, fled to Holland in 1608 to escape persecution. After several false starts, the group of Puritans, known as the Pilgrim Fathers, set sail for America from Plymouth on 16th September 1620 aboard the "Mayflower".

IRISH TROUBLES

Following the collapse of the Irish rebellion, led by the Earls of Tyrone and Tyrconnel, Ulster was colonised by English and Scottish Protestants. Although England and Ireland had long been at war (albeit intermittently), it was this act, perhaps more than any other, that led to the religious and political divisions within Ireland, laying the foundations for the modern "troubles".

Bates — Robert Winter — Christopher Wright — John Wright — Thomas Percy — Guido (Guy) Fawkes — Robert Catesby — Thomas Winter

THE GUNPOWDER PLOT

James I was an unpopular king, particularly with the Catholics, who petitioned him for fairer treatment but were ignored. There had already been several failed attempts to depose him in 1603, but in 1605 a group of Catholic nobles attempted to assassinate the king and destroy his Protestant Parliament. One of the conspirators was an explosives expert, one Guido (Guy) Fawkes. The plotters made the fatal mistake of warning fellow Catholics of the intended day of the explosion. They were arrested and the gang were imprisoned, tortured and executed.

📖 ARTS & LITERATURE   ● BATTLES   ⚖ CRIME & PUNISHMENT

CHARLES I (1625–49)

Charles I was another man who was not born to be king, only inheriting the crown following the death of his elder brother, Henry. An intelligent man of diminutive stature, he also had a slight stammer, reflecting his shyness and lack of self-confidence. Charles was very much aware of his responsibilities as king and performed his duties with quiet dignity. Like his father, James I, Charles believed uncompromisingly in the "Divine Right of Kings", which frequently brought him into conflict with Parliament. Following the death of his advisor George Villiers, Duke of Buckingham, Charles decided to dissolve Parliament, ruling on his own for 11 years, between 1629-40. His rule became increasingly difficult and he was forced to recall Parliament, but Charles quarrelled with Parliament again and tried to arrest five members. This move was to lead to civil war.

THE CIVIL WAR

Although England had frequently witnessed civil wars, these were mostly local and regional. The Civil War of 1642-49 was the first time the entire country had ranged itself into two distinct factions between King and Parliament, and the first time since the Battle of Bosworth in 1485 that fellow Englishmen had taken up arms against one another. The Civil War was a turning point in English constitutional history. Even though the monarchy was restored in 1660 following England's brief period as a republic, it was never again able to wield such power and became much more accountable.

EXECUTION

Charles remains the only British monarch to have been formally charged with treason and executed. Parliament tried the king for waging war against his own people. The trial began on 20th January 1649 and lasted just one week. Found guilty, Charles was beheaded three days later.

ENGLAND DECLARED A REPUBLIC

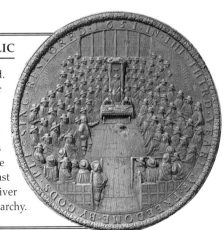

Britain's only brush with republicanism was short-lived. The dominant figure throughout the Civil War was Oliver Cromwell and, although he devised a new (and in many ways fairer) system of government, it was never fully democratic and it disintegrated when he died. Although a brilliant leader, the strength of Cromwell's leadership lay in his personal qualities and not in the reforms he introduced. Cromwell was offered the crown of England in 1657, but he refused, saying he was against the principle of hereditary rule. Within two years of Oliver Cromwell's death, Parliament recalled the monarchy.

 EXPLORATION   GOVERNMENT   ✝ RELIGION

CHARLES II (1660–1685)

Following the execution of his father and his own unsuccessful attempts to ascend the throne, Charles II was forced into exile in Europe. Although technically still king, Charles had little money and for 11 years lived a frugal existence. When Oliver Cromwell died in 1658 the Commonwealth began to collapse. To avert another civil war, Parliament asked the exiled king to return to England. He arrived in London on on his 30th birthday.

Cromwell's body was exhumed and hanged at Tyburn, but otherwise the Restoration passed without further recriminations and was greeted with wild enthusiasm by the repressed population. When Charles was invited to become king, he married Catherine of Braganza, from Portugal. It was a loveless marriage and Charles, known as the Merry Monarch, took an estimated 17 mistresses. He had 14 illegitimate children, but he had none with his wife and so left no heir.

JAMES II (1685-1688)

Like all the Stuarts, James was a proud, haughty man, who believed strongly in the doctrine of the "Divine Right of Kings" (*see page 20*). He was the second son of Charles I and acceded on the death of his brother. James spent much of his early life in government office and was made Lord High Admiral, serving in the Dutch wars. He aroused considerable opposition from Parliament because of his strong Catholic views. Although tall, handsome and by all accounts well-mannered, because of his arrogance he never won the popular support of his people.

✞ RESTORATION OF CATHOLICISM

James converted to Catholicism in the 1660s, much to the disapproval of Parliament, who removed him from high office and tried, unsuccessfully, to prevent his succession to the throne. He declared from the outset that he intended to restore Catholicism as the main religion of Britain. To help him achieve this James increased the standing army from 6,000 to 30,000, replacing many of the Protestant officers with Catholics.

THE GLORIOUS REVOLUTION

In 1688 Parliament invited William of Orange, ruler of Holland and James's son-in-law, to restore liberties to England. He landed in Devon with an invasion force. Although William was not a popular figure, James II had little support himself and the Dutchman marched on London to force the king's deposition in a virtually bloodless coup. When faced with the choice of accepting Parliament's demands or deposition, James refused to compromise his ideals. He was deposed on 23rd December 1688 and forced into exile in France, where he died in 1701.

📖 ARTS & LITERATURE　　🔴 BATTLES　　⚖ CRIME & PUNISHMENT

WILLIAM III & MARY II
(1689–1702)

The deposition of James II was a significant turning point in the history of England's monarchy. It was now a Parliamentary institution, bound by the rules set by government. When William of Orange was offered the throne, he had to accept Parliament's conditions, namely that he ruled jointly with James's eldest daughter Mary (whom William had married 12 years before) and that he must agree to constitutional restraints on royal power. William accepted these conditions, though he had little interest in England, using the situation to strengthen Holland's position against the mighty power of France. William was a man of slight build and was never very popular with the English, unlike Mary, who was much liked. She died from smallpox at the premature age of 32. William died eight years later in a riding accident.

BILL OF RIGHTS

Early in 1689 Parliament drew up the Declaration of Rights. It is usually seen as the second most important piece of constitutional legislation after the Magna Carta, and reduced royal power considerably. It stated that no Catholic could ever become the ruling monarch and that Parliament needed to agree to any changes in taxes and laws.

SCOTTISH REBELLION

When Charles II was restored to the throne in 1660, Scotland was once again accepted as a separate kingdom. When William III came to the throne, however, the Scots saw this independence threatened and many rebelled against him in favour of James II, who was from the royal Scottish family of Stuart. The rebellion was put down later in 1689 and the Scots were made to swear and oath of allegiance to William.

BATTLE OF THE BOYNE

Following James II's deposition by William of Orange, the Irish Catholics sided with James in a rebellion. The Irish Protestants, who had mostly settled around Ulster, sided with William. On 1st July 1690 a pitched battle was fought, but William's superior forces quickly overran James's army, though William graciously allowed James to escape into exile.

ANNE (1702–1714)

Anne was the second daughter of James II and Anne Hyde. She succeeded William III, her brother-in-law, in 1702, when he died without leaving an heir. Anne was the last Stuart monarch to rule England. Her short reign was a strong one, bolstered by a series of military victories on the Continent, which established Britain as the most powerful country in Europe. During this period, Parliament consolidated its constitutional successes, making the British government one of the strongest and most democratic institutions then known and the envy of other European countries. Although attractive in her youth, in later years Anne suffered from numerous ailments, including obesity and gout, and had to be carried about in a chair. She had 18 pregnancies but all of her children died in childbirth or infancy.

ACT OF UNION

When James IV of Scotland was crowned as James I of England, the crowns of those two countries were united, but Scotland retained its own parliament. In 1707, however, the Act of Union was passed, uniting the governments of the two countries and the Scottish parliament was abolished. Scotland sent 45 members and 16 peers to the new Parliament of Great Britain in London.

ACT OF SETTLEMENT

In 1701 the Act of Settlement was passed which ensured that the line of succession should pass to the Electress Sophia of Hanover, or her heirs, who were Protestants and distantly related to the Stuarts. In the event, the crown passed to James I's great-grandson, who became George I, rather than to Anne's Catholic half-brother James, the "Old Pretender".

 EXPLORATION   GOVERNMENT   ✝ RELIGION

THE HANOVERIANS

1714 ~ 1910

*W*hen Anne died without leaving an heir, succession to the throne passed to George of Hanover, great-grandson of James I and Anne's closest relative. In 1701 the Act of Settlement had been passed which ensured that a Catholic monarch could never again sit on the British throne, but George's accession was not a popular choice. This was especially true in Scotland where rebellion broke out in 1715 to place a Stuart back on the throne. This Jacobite rebellion was led by the son of James II, but the revolt was soon put down.

GEORGE I (1714-27)

George I (left) was the first Hanoverian monarch of Britain. He had little interest in Britain and only spoke German, so it became necessary for many of his governmental duties to be transferred to Parliament and his ministers. Sir Robert Walpole, a member of the Whig (Liberal) party, took the opportunity of increasing the power and influence of the House of Commons. In 1721 he had made himself the most powerful person in Parliament, and became, in effect, the first Prime Minister. George had married Sophia Dorothea, the beautiful but arrogant daughter of a German duke, before becoming king. It was a loveless marriage and after she bore him two children they went their separate ways. In his heart Hanover remained George's home and he died on his way there in 1727.

CAROLINE OF BRANDENBURG-ANSBACH

George married Caroline in 1705 and together they had ten children. She remained faithful to him, even though he had numerous affairs. George never remarried after Caroline's death in 1737. She was plump, but not unattractive, and possessed great charm and intelligence, striking up a life-long (though strictly professional) friendship with Robert Walpole.

GEORGE II (1727–60)

Under the expert guidance of Walpole, the first third of George II's reign was one of peace and great prosperity in which the British Empire acquired considerable new domains. The Prime Minister skilfully steered Britain away from all wars in Europe, but after he retired from politics, the remainder of George's reign was spent in one conflict or another, including war with Spain and two separate conflicts with France. George himself was not an inspiring monarch or indeed a very likeable or interesting man. His only distinction was his military record and his passion for music.

THE SECOND JACOBITE REBELLION (1745)

While the first Jacobite rebellion (1715) was quickly crushed, the second uprising was a much more serious attempt to place the Catholic Stuarts back on the throne. The word Jacobite comes from the Latin word for James –Jacobus – and is the name adopted by the supporters of James II and his heirs. This second rising was led by Charles Edward Stuart, known as "Bonnie Prince Charlie". He achieved early success against the English at the Battle of Prestonpans in July 1745, but by the following April he was defeated. Charles escaped to exile in France (aided by Flora Macdonald) and died penniless in 1788.

● BATTLE OF CULLODEN

The hopes and dreams of the Jacobite rebels came to an end at the Battle of Culloden in April 1746. The English, under the Duke of Cumberland, inflicted a massive defeat on the Scots, thus ending the Stuart claim to the throne once and for all. For many years after, even the wearing of kilts and the playing of bagpipes was punishable by death.

⧉ EXPANSION OF THE BRITISH EMPIRE

James Wolfe was a courageous and capable commander in the British army. He led the attack on Quebec in 1759, which secured Canada as part of the Empire. Robert Clive was doing likewise in India. In 1757 he won the Battle of Plessey, adding India to the Empire. He was appointed governor of Bengal but was hated by the Indians and was censured for misgovernment.

GEORGE III (1760–1820)

George III was the first of the Hanoverian monarchs to be born in England. He succeeded to the throne in 1760 on the death of his grandfather, George II, and took an immediate interest in affairs of state. Unlike his two predecessors, he regarded himself as English and the people warmed to his simple, direct manner. Geroge's long reign spanned almost the entire period now termed the "Industrial Revolution" and saw many changes, but he is perhaps best remembered for the loss of the American colonies in 1783. George always regarded himself as an ordinary man. He was very hard-working and took a strong interest in government. From an early age he also showed a keen interest in farming and liked to chat to workers on the royal farms, earning him the nickname "Farmer George". From 1788 George suffered periods of illness and mental instability. He was kept locked away and in 1811 his son was made Prince Regent. Modern research suggests that George was not mad but suffering from *porphyria*, a hereditary disease that causes mental confusion.

A DEVOTED QUEEN

On 8th September 1761 George married Charlotte of Mecklenburg-Strelitz. The early years of their marriage were very happy and they had 15 children. Charlotte was intelligent and vivacious in her youth, but became quite obese in later life. She grew to love George and remained devoted to him throughout his earlier bouts of illness, but gradually grew away from him in later life. Sadly, the king did not recognise Charlotte when she died in 1818 aged 75.

⧉ EXPLORATION   ◫ GOVERNMENT   ✝ RELIGION

GEORGE IV (1820–30)

In 1811 George III's son became Regent, as Prince George, taking over many of the constitutional roles of his father, who was considered unfit to govern. On his father's death in 1820, Prince George became George IV. Having spent the better part of his life in his father's shadow, George IV's reign was a comparatively short one and he proved himself to be an unworthy successor. Always prone to excesses, particularly during his Regency, he changed from a handsome, popular prince into a debauched and obese caricature of his former self. As part of a deal to get Parliament to pay off his mounting debts, George had to marry his cousin, Caroline of Brunswick, in 1795. It was a loveless match and George refused to allow her to be present at his Coronation.

MRS. FITZHERBERT

The Act of Settlement, passed in 1701, forbade George (heir to the throne) to marry a Catholic. However, he married his Catholic mistress, Maria Fitzherbert, in secret in 1785. The marriage was never officially recognised.

WILLIAM IV (1830–7)

As the third son of George III, William could never have expected to become king and only did so, at the age of 64, on the death of his brother, George. William had joined the navy at the age of 13 and quickly rose to the rank of captain. He became popularly known as the "Sailor King". Less complimentary was the nickname "Silly Billy", a name he earned because of his forthright manner and propensity to make tactless remarks. These rather unstatesmanlike traits were combined with sometimes inept but nevertheless enthusiastic attempts at government. To be fair, William was likeable and lacked his brother's extravagances, which endeared him to the people. His short reign was one of great constitutional change and political reform.

📓 FIRST REFORM ACT

William's reign saw a number of important legal and political reforms including the First Reform Act (1837), which attempted to reform the voting system. The vote was extended to property owners, land owners and some tenants, and a fairer, more proportional system of allocating parliamentary seats was introduced.

DOROTHEA JORDAN

Although he never married her, William lived with his actress mistress Dorothea Jordan for 21 years. She bore him 10 illegitimate children. Financial pressures forced William to marry Adelaide of Saxe-Meiningen in 1818 but she bore him no children and so William had no legitimate heir.

📖 ARTS & LITERATURE   💣 BATTLES   ⚖ CRIME & PUNISHMENT

VICTORIA (1837–1901)

Victoria came to the throne at the age of 18 after her uncle, William IV, died childless in 1837. She was fifth in line to the throne and the likelihood of her succeeding seemed very remote. Although young, Victoria came to the throne with enthusiasm and consulted frequently with her ministers. One of the first dilemmas facing her was that of marriage. She was advised to marry as soon as possible and agreed to meet her cousin, Prince Albert of Saxe-Coburg-Gotha. Victoria married Prince Albert in 1840 when they were both 20 years old. It was a genuine love match and together they had nine children. Often seen as a stern and serious woman, she was supposedly a jovial person who was amused by her children and enjoyed family life. Victoria became England's longest reigning monarch and, by the time of her death, she was ruler of the largest empire the world had ever seen.

PRINCE ALBERT

Albert was intelligent, talented and proved himself to be an able administrator. He designed the royal houses of Osborne and Balmoral and was the instigator of the Great Exhibition, believing that by promoting industry it would generate more work and so help the poor. Proceeds from the profits were used to fund various public institutes, including many of London's museums. When Albert died from typhoid in 1861 at the age of 42, the queen went into mourning for 13 years and had a number of buildings and monuments erected in his honour.

THE GREAT EMPIRE

Because it was not conceived as a single plan, the British Empire grew very slowly, allowing new colonies to be gradually brought under British control. During Elizabeth I's reign, it consisted only of a handful of settlements in North America and grew hardly at all during the 17th century. In the 19th century it began to grow rapidly, coming to the full height of its power under Victoria. During this time, the British empire covered one quarter of the world's land mass.

EDWARD VII (1901–10)

Edward VII was the eldest son of Queen Victoria and Prince Albert. His relationship with his parents, especially his mother, was often strained. Even though Edward took over many of her administrative duties as Prince of Wales, Victoria did not entirely trust his judgement and often excluded him from any real involvement in governmental matters. Edward lived life to the full (which earned him both popularity and derision) and had several mistresses, even though he was said to be happily married to Princess Alexandra, of Denmark, for many years.

ENTENTE CORDIALE

The historic "Entente Cordiale" (or "cordial understanding") was an agreement between Britain and France to settle territorial disputes. It was further extended in 1908 to include Russia. On a visit to Paris in 1903 Edward VII paved the way for the political discussions that followed. The major powers of Europe seemed to be on a collision course and the agreement was intended to settle land disputes and avert war by forming an opposing group to balance the power of the Triple Alliance between Germany, Italy and Austria-Hungary.

 EXPLORATION   GOVERNMENT   ✝ RELIGION

THE WINDSORS

1910 ~ PRESENT DAY

GEORGE V (1910–36)

*W*hen he came to the throne, George V changed the family name to Windsor because of the anti-German feeling at the time. So began a new dynastic line, which continues today with the present queen, Elizabeth II. Elizabeth is the 56th monarch since Alfred the Great was made King of England in 899. Her reign is the fourth longest in the history of Britain and, despite many challenges, she has gained the respect and love of her people.

As has often been the case with the British monarchy, George V was not born to be king. He came to the throne on the death of his brother, Edward. George's reign was marked by social unrest, changes to the constitution that curbed the powers of the House of Lords, and a devastating world war. It was a time when the monarchy stood for continuity and stability, and George V, supported by his wife Mary, proved to be a dignified and admired head of State. He made the first Christmas broadcast to the nation to try to lift the people's spirits, a tradition still performed today.

WORLD WAR I

The First World War began more as a trade war between European powers, rather than (as a popularly believed) a bid for world domination. What started out with Germany flexing its muscles and bullying its neighbours, soon escalated into world-wide warfare. Despite being Kaiser Wilhelm's cousin, George V fully supported the government's stand against him when Germany invaded Belgium in 1914. But the scale and length of the war could never have been imagined.

INSTRUMENT OF ABDICATION

When Edward VIII announced his intention to abdicate, the Prime Minister, Stanley Baldwin, had to quickly draw up a formal abdication notice, which was rushed through Parliament. The following day Edward explained his reasons over the radio.

EDWARD VIII (1936)

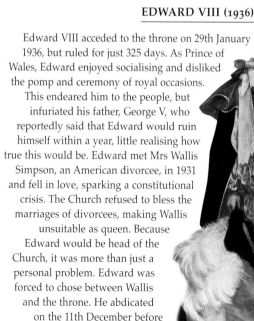

Edward VIII acceded to the throne on 29th January 1936, but ruled for just 325 days. As Prince of Wales, Edward enjoyed socialising and disliked the pomp and ceremony of royal occasions. This endeared him to the people, but infuriated his father, George V, who reportedly said that Edward would ruin himself within a year, little realising how true this would be. Edward met Mrs Wallis Simpson, an American divorcee, in 1931 and fell in love, sparking a constitutional crisis. The Church refused to bless the marriages of divorcees, making Wallis unsuitable as queen. Because Edward would be head of the Church, it was more than just a personal problem. Edward was forced to chose between Wallis and the throne. He abdicated on the 11th December before he had been crowned.

ARTS & LITERATURE   BATTLES   CRIME & PUNISHMENT

GEORGE VI (1936–52)

When Edward VIII abdicated, the crown passed to his brother, Albert, who assumed the name George VI on his coronation. He was an intensely shy man, nervous in public, and suffered from an acute stammer. He is said to have confessed, "I never wanted this to happen. I'm only a naval officer, it's the only thing I know about". Nevertheless, George proved himself more than equal to the task, especially during the Second World War. He refused to leave England and made several morale-boosting visits to the troops abroad. Throughout his reign, his wife, Elizabeth, remained by his side as a constant support. After his unexpected death in 1952, she continued to offer her support to her daughter, the young Queen Elizabeth II. Elizabeth, the Queen Mother, as she became known, continued her public duties right up until her death in 2002 at the age of 101. Her popularity never wavered and she died a much-loved royal.

ELIZABETH II (1952–TODAY)

Elizabeth came to the throne at the age of 25 on the unexpected death of her father. As Princess, she won great acclaim by joining the Auxiliary Transport Service during the Second World War. Since then she has gained great respect for her unwavering devotion to her royal duties. The role of monarch has reduced dramatically over the centuries, but Elizabeth presides over many official and State occasions and remains supreme head of the British armed services.

WORLD WAR II

After the First World War, the blight of economic recession had fallen upon Europe. Germany was hit the hardest, which paved the way for social unrest. When the fanatical Adolf Hitler appeared, inciting the people with his speeches of world domination, they willingly followed. He built up the German army and then invaded Poland on September 1st, 1939. War was declared on 3rd September. The final death toll after hostilities ended in 1945 exceeded 40 million.

ELIZABETH'S FAMILY

Elizabeth is supported by Prince Philip, whom she married in 1947, and they have four children. In recent years, her children have been the cause of her greatest challenges as a monarch. The failure of the marriage of her son and heir, Prince Charles, and Diana, Princess of Wales, threatened to unstabilise the monarchy. It was a very public and bitter breakdown, and public sympathies appeared to lie with Diana. When she died in a car crash in 1997, the whole country was shocked and grieving. Not for the first time during her reign, Elizabeth experienced hostility from the public. This has led to a more media-friendly, informal approach, shown during the Queen's Golden Jubilee Year in 2002.

THE FUTURE OF THE MONARCHY

Prince Charles (shown here during his marriage to Diana) faces a number of challenges when he accedes to the throne, not least because of his relationship with Camilla Parker-Bowles, a divorcee and the woman he was publicly exposed as having an affair with during his marriage. Charles has voiced controversial views, but in keeping with modern times and sympathetic with the mood of the people, he has been unafraid to show his personal side and his genuine love for his children and his country.

EXPLORATION   GOVERNMENT   RELIGION

THE ROYAL FAMILY TREE

KINGS & QUEENS OF SCOTLAND LINE OF SUCCESSION

KENNETH MacALPIN - 834-859
DONALD I - 859-863
CONSTANTINE I - 863-877
AEDH - 877-878
EOCHA - 878-889
DONALD II - 889-900
CONSTANTINE II - 900-942
MALCOLM I - 942-954
INDULPHUS - 954-962
DUFF - 962-967
CULEAN - 967-971
KENNETH II - 971-995
CONSTANTINE III - 995-997
KENNETH III - 997-1005
MALCOLM II - 1005-1034
DUNCAN I - 1034-1040

MACBETH - 1040-1057
LULACH - 1057-1058
MALCOLM III - 1058-1093
DONALD III - 1093-1094
& 1094-1097
DUNCAN II - 1094
EDGAR - 1097-1107
ALEXANDER I - 1107-1124
DAVID I - 1124-1153
MALCOLM IV - 1153-1165
WILLIAM THE LION - 1165-1214
ALEXANDER II - 1214-1249
ALEXANDER III - 1249-1286
MARGARET OF NORWAY - 1286-90
JOHN BALLIOL - 1292-96 (Edward I of England - 1296-1306)

ROBERT I (Bruce) - 1306-1329
DAVID II (Bruce) - 1329-1332
EDWARD BALLIOL - 1332-56
DAVID II (Bruce) - 1356-1371
ROBERT II - 1371-1390
ROBERT III - 1390-1406
JAMES I - 1406-1437
JAMES II - 1437-1460
JAMES III - 1460-1488
JAMES IV - 1488-1513
JAMES V - 1513-1542
MARY - 1542-1567
JAMES VI - 1567-1625
(who became James I of England and the countries were united)

THE NORMANS 1066 - 1154

WILLIAM I 1066-1087 m Matilda of Flanders

HENRY I 1100-1135
m Matilda of Scotland

ADELA
m Stephen, Count of Blois

WILLIAM II 1087-1100

MATILDA m
Geoffrey, Count of Anjou

STEPHEN 1135-1154

THE PLANTAGENETS 1154 - 1399

HENRY II 1154-1189 m Eleanor of Aquitaine

RICHARD I 1189-1199

JOHN 1199-1216 m Isabel of Angouleme

HENRY III 1216-1272 m Eleanor of Provence

EDWARD I 1272-1307 m Eleanor of Castile

EDWARD II 1307-1327 m Isabella of France

EDWARD III 1327-1377 m Philippa of Hainault

EDWARD PRINCE OF WALES
(The Black Prince) m Joan of Kent

RICHARD II 1377-1399

HOUSE OF LANCASTER 1399 -1461

JOHN OF GAUNT m1 Blanche of Lancaster   m2 Constance of Castile
m3 Katharine Swynford

HENRY IV 1399-1413 m Mary de Bohun

HENRY V 1413-1422 m1 Katherine of France   m2 Owen Tudor

HENRY VI 1422-1471

EDWARD, PRINCE OF WALES

JOHN BEAUFORT Earl of Somerset

JOHN BEAUFORT Duke of Somerset

EDMUND DUKE OF YORK

RICHARD, EARL OF CAMBRIDGE

RICHARD DUKE OF YORK

THE HOUSE OF YORK 1461 - 1485

EDWARD IV 1461-1483   RICHARD III 1483-1485

EDWARD V

TUDOR MONARCHS 1485-1603

EDMUND m Margaret
TUDOR   Beaufort

HENRY VII   m   Elizabeth
1485-1509   of York

MARGARET TUDOR m James IV of Scotland

MARY QUEEN OF SCOTS m Henry Stuart

THE STUARTS 1603-1714

JAMES I (VI of Scotland) 1603-1625 m Anne of Denmark

HENRY FREDRICK, PRINCE OF WALES d.1612

CHARLES I 1625-1649 m Henrietta Maria of France d. 1669

MARY m William, Prince of Orange

CHARLES II 1649-1685 m Catherine of Braganza d.1705

JAMES II 1685-1688 d. 1701 m Anne Hyde d.1671

WILLIAM III 1689-1702 m MARY II 1689-1694

ANNE 1702-1714 m George of Denmark

ELIZABETH d.1662 m Frederick V, Elector Palatine of the Rhine

m1 Catherine of Aragon (div 1533)
MARY I 1553-1558

(d.1536)
ELIZABETH I 1558-1603

(d.1537)
EDWARD VI 1547-1553

m5 Catherine Howard (d. 1542)
m6 Catherine Parr (d. 1548)

SOPHIA d.1612 m Ernest Augustus, Elector of Hanover d.1698

RUPERT OF THE RHINE d.1682

THE HANOVARIANS 1714 - 1910

GEORGE I 1714-1727 m Sophia Dorothea of Zelle d.1726

GEORGE II 1727-1760 m Caroline of Anspach d.1737

FREDERICK LEWIS, PRINCE OF WALES d.1751 m Augusta of Saxe-Gotha d.1772

GEORGE III 1760-1820 m Sophia Charlotte of Mecklenburg-Strelitz d.1818

EDWARD, DUKE OF KENT d.1820 m Victoria of Saxe-Coburg-Saalfeld d.1861

VICTORIA 1837-1901 m Albert of Saxe-Coburg-Gotha, Prince Consort d.1861

EDWARD VII 1901-1910

WILLIAM IV 1830-1837 m Adelaide of Saxe-Meiningen 1792-1849

CHARLOTTE d.1819

ELIZABETH d.1821

GEORGE IV 1820-1830 m Caroline of Brunswick

CHARLOTTE d.1817

HOUSE OF WINDSOR 1910-

GEORGE V 1910-1936

EDWARD VIII, DUKE OF WINDSOR 1936 (d.1972) m Elizabeth Bowes-Lyon

GEORGE VI 1936-1952 m Elizabeth Bowes-Lyon

ELIZABETH II 1952-

KINGS & QUEENS OF ENGLAND
(Britain from 1603) LINE OF SUCCESSION

ECGBERHT - 827-839	EDWARD II - 1307-1327
AETHELWULF - 839-866	EDWARD III - 1327-1377
AETHELRED I - 866-871	RICHARD II - 1377-1399
ALFRED THE GREAT - 871-900	HENRY IV - 1399-1413
EDWARD THE ELDER - 900-924	HENRY V - 1413-1422
ATHELSTAN - 924-940	HENRY VI - 1422-1471
EDMUND I - 940-946	EDWARD IV - 1461-1483
EADRED I - 946-955	EDWARD V - 1483
EDWY - 955-959	RICHARD III - 1483-1485
EDGAR THE PEACEABLE - 959-975	HENRY VII - 1485-1509
EDWARD THE MARTYR - 975-978	HENRY VIII - 1509-1547
AETHELRED II - 978-1013 & 1014-1016	EDWARD VI - 1547-1553
SWEYN (Dane) - 1013-1014	MARY I - 1553-1558
EDMUND IRONSIDE - 1016	ELIZABETH I - 1558-1603
CANUTE (Dane) - 1016-1035	JAMES I - 1603-1625
HAROLD HAREFOOT (Dane) - 1035-1040	CHARLES I - 1625-1649
HARTHACANUTE (Dane) - 1040-1042	CHARLES II - 1649-1685
EDWARD THE CONFESSOR - 1042-1066	JAMES II - 1685-1688
HAROLD II - 1066	WILLIAM III & MARY II - 1689-1702
WILLIAM I (the Conqueror) - 1066-1087	ANNE - 1702-1714
WILLIAM II - 1087-1100	GEORGE I - 1714-1727
HENRY I - 1100-1135	GEORGE II - 1727-1760
STEPHEN - 1135-1154	GEORGE III - 1760-1820
HENRY II - 1154-1189	GEORGE IV - 1820-1830
RICHARD I - 1189-1199	WILLIAM IV - 1830-1837
JOHN - 1199-1216	VICTORIA - 1837-1901
HENRY III - 1216-1272	EDWARD VII - 1901-1910
EDWARD I - 1272-1307	GEORGE V - 1910-1936
	EDWARD VIII - 1936
	GEORGE VI - 1936-1952
	ELIZABETH II - 1952-today

• The Normans enjoyed hunting so much they gave over large tracts of land for the sport. They chased stags, wild boar and even wolves, which were not yet extinct in England.

• Stories of Robin Hood were circulating as early as 1262. The legend told of a disinherited Saxon nobleman who led a band of outlaws against the tyranny of a corrupt ruler.

•In his later years, Henry VIII was obsessed with his personal safety. Whilst staying at Allington Castle, the king actually had himself walled in every night!

• Sir Walter Raleigh was responsible for introducing tobacco to England. But he also brought home potatoes, chillies and other exotic foods from his trips to the far flung corners of the world.

• In the 17th century, England's population was decimated by a dreadful new disease called the plague. Its other name, the Black Death, testified to its deadliness. Over half of the population who caught the disease died within five days. The plague still exists today in hot countries, but can be treated with antibiotics.

• During the Second World War, George V refused to leave London, even when Buckingham Palace was bombed in 1940. He wanted to take an active role in the war, but was dissuaded from doing so by the Prime Minister Winston Churchill. However, the King did instigate the George Cross and the George Medal to reward civilian heroes in during times of war.

A C K N O W L E D G E M E N T S

This Series is dedicated to J. Allan Twiggs whose enthusiasm for British History has inspired these four books.

A CIP catalogue record for this book is available from the British Library. ISBN 1 86007 398 0

Printed in China

Acknowledgements: Picture Credits t=top, b=bottom, c=centre, l=left, r=right, OFC=outside front cover, IFC=inside front cover, IBC=inside back cover, OBC=outside back cover.

Ancient Art and Architecture: 4c, 5t, 6b, 7r, 11t, 11c, 11b, 12tl, 14t, 18cr, 21b, 24b. Archiv Fur Konst (London): 22b. Bridgeman Art Library: 4b, 5b, 8tl & 32c, 10t, 12b, 14b, 15tl, 15cr, 16t, 25t, 27t, 27cl. Corbis: 29c. Mary Evans Picture Library: 3tl, 3tr, 3cr, 5cr, 6l, 7c, 8cr, 8b, 9t, 9b, 13l, 14b, 15tr, 18t, 19tl, 19tr, 20t, 20b, 22tr, 23tl, 23tr, 23b, 24l, 26cl, 26bl, 27b, 28tl, 28bl, 28br, 29tl. Image Select: 2bl. National Maritime Museum: 25br, 25bl, 26br. National Portrait Gallery: 16bl, 21r, 22tl, 26t. Stirling Castle: 19b.

Every effort has been made to trace the copyright holders and we apologise in advance for any unintentional omissions. We would be pleased to insert the appropriate acknowledgement in any subsequent edition of this publication.